Improve Your Self With Yoga Techniques

ASHOK WAHI'S
THE MISSING PEACE™

ASHOK WAHI
AND
STEFANI PAPPAS / MEGAN O' MALLEY

PRINCETON DESIGN GROUP, INC.
HILLSBOROUGH, NEW JERSEY

Business Consultant; Michael Schenkel, Ph. D.

Book Design by; Vincent Golden, Golden Associates, Hillsborough, New Jersey

Illustrations by; Roger Long, Senior Art Teacher

Lead Proofreader; Virginia Gittelman, Ed. D.

Marketing Consultant; Francine DiFilippo, DeFilippo Business Services, Sarasota, Florida

Photographs by; Lloyd and Sunny Yellen, Sunny Yellen Photography, Piscataway, New Jersey

Yoga artists; Michael Flynn, Dr. Frederick L. Kingsbury, Stefani Pappas

Printed at; Cottonwood Printing Co., Albuquerque, New Mexico

Library of Congress Cataloging-in-Publication Data

Wahi, Ashok / Pappas, Stefani /O'Malley, Megan
The Missing Peace ™
p. cm.
Printed in the United States of America
The Missing Peace ™, Improve Your Golf with Yoga Techniques
Authors: Ashok Wahi, Stefani Pappas, and Megan O'Malley
Concept Created by Ashok Wahi
Golf – Training   2. Exercise   3. Yoga Techniques
I. Wahi, Pappas, O'Malley.
II. Princeton Design Group, Inc.
© 2001 by Ashok Wahi, et. al.
ISBN 0-9708284-1-1

This book is available at special discounts for bulk purchase. Special editions or book excerpts can also be created to specification. For details contact:
Princeton Design Group, Inc.
Web site: www.themissingpeace.net
FAX 908-359-9137

Publisher: Princeton Design Group, Inc.
601 Omni Drive,
Hillsborough, NJ 08844 (USA)

DEDICATION

With the kindness and blessings of our Satguru (Master), this and all our efforts are dedicated to the betterment of mankind.

Neelu and Ashok Wahi

FOREWORD

Read *The Missing Peace* ™ and learn to improve your game of golf through the practice of hatha yoga. From the recreational player to the professional, all golfers can benefit from this unique book that shows you how the mental and physical conditioning of Yoga brings focus to the game of golf.

You don't have to believe in gravity to know that what goes up must come down. Whether or not you believe in the science, yoga can positively affect your golf game.

Hatha yoga integrates the mind and the body, an essential feature for success in any sport. Alignment, strength, balance, and flexibility of the body all develop in a way superior to any other physical conditioning program. Further, the mind-body connection explained in this book allows the player to acquire the mental discipline needed for relaxed, healthy, and enjoyable play. *The Missing Peace* can also bring relaxation and enjoyment to your life, generally.

At a business dinner a few years ago, I heard someone ask, "How often do you play golf?" "Maybe three or four times a week," came the reply. The response was, "So, what do you do to relax?"

For many, the discipline involved in playing golf may not come naturally. If not natural, relaxation techniques should be learned for the benefit of the golfer's game. Without techniques for mastering the psyche in the game of golf, you may be frustrated, stressed and disappointed with your performance, suffering at the mercy of mind and emotions.

With this book, you, the golfer, can learn to relax while playing, so that you can achieve your potential. Yoga can teach you to trust muscle memory, accessing practice through visualization and relaxation. The moment-to-moment focus of yoga practice will encourage you to let the game and life unfold.

Described in this book are the yoga techniques that provide tangible gains in lowering your score. We promise success that you can feel and measure. As you practice the techniques explained in this book, you will learn to be more patient and derive more enjoyment from the game of golf.

Based upon extensive research, the 45-minute exercise plan presented and explained in this book can be done any time of the day, anywhere, and any number of times a week. It includes a 9-minute warm up that should be done before every golf game.

Illustrations and pictures facilitate understanding of all the techniques. *The Missing Peace* is all you need!

Look for other titles in the series.

CONTENTS

PART ONE

PART TWO

PART THREE

The information in this book is derived from the experience of its authors and co-authors. It is intended for educational purposes only. The publisher as well as the authors, co-authors, associates, endorsers, consultants and affiliates accept absolutely no liability for the use of this information. Any information given herein is not intended as a replacement for expert advice, teaching and guidance.

PART ONE

CHAPTER 1: GOLF AND THE MISSING "PIECE"

Some recent immigrants to the US were being tested on their knowledge of the fifty states. They were actually being prepared before their interviews for further education and jobs. One of the quizzes involved a jigsaw puzzle. The puzzle was a map of the United States with fifty different pieces representing all the states in the country. The candidates were given five minutes to put the puzzle together. Most of the people struggled to put a dozen of the states together. They seemed exhausted with that effort. A few reached thirty states, but the task remained far from completion.

One of the calmer individuals took the puzzle, then observed and absorbed the assignment at hand. He viewed the bigger picture. After assessing the challenge carefully, he went to the task. To every examiner's surprise, he put the entire puzzle back together with a minute and a half to spare.

The puzzle pieces were all in the right place. The examiners were astounded to see the puzzle completed perfectly.

"How do you know so much about the geography of the US?" questioned one examiner.

"I don't know anything about it," he responded casually.

The examiners' suspense grew, and the candidate explained himself. "I am not familiar with where different states appear on the map, but in my observation, I discovered that there's a picture of a human being on the reverse of the puzzle. Once I recognized that, every piece fell in its place. I do not know where the states should be, but I do know where the head should be. The other limbs take their respective places. Feet stay on the ground. Once that was clear to me, then it was apparent where the shoes go. By putting the human being together in the background, I was able to put the entire map together in the foreground!"

A great many of the millions of people who play golf are making an effort to improve their game by putting together a puzzle on the surface. They have managed to ignore the simpler, bigger picture just waiting to be discovered in the background. Once yoga becomes part of a golfer's life, every puzzle piece falls into place.

Beginning with your first breath in yoga, you can learn to unravel and deconstruct barriers to your success in golf. Breathing forms the connection between mind and body. Breathing through obstacles keeps the mind calm, creating patience and acceptance of self. Yoga helps the player reduce both inside and outside distractions. Further, by making subtle adjustments in poses, the golfer can create an individual mental focus. Yoga's attention to mental discipline makes it perfect for cross training with golf.

The practice of yoga not only affects the quality of play, but also helps to prevent injuries and speeds the player's recovery. Strong flexible muscles are less likely to be sore after play because efficient use of the muscles creates action that is focused and relaxed. Greater energy and vitality at the end of the game means further enjoyment of the experience.

Yoga addresses both the mental and physical aspects of the game. The poses are not only a physical activity, but they are also a mental discipline. During the poses the golfer explores the subtleties of movement and feeling.

Whether playing golf as recreation or playing golf in competition, golf is a game to be enjoyed.

Chapter 2: What Do We Know About Golf?

On the simplest level, golf is a game in which a ball is struck with a club from the tee through the fairway, avoiding the rough, to a putting green. The object of the game is to complete each of eighteen holes in the fewest possible strokes.

Fueled by the recent success and tremendous popularity of younger Professional Golf Association (PGA) stars such as Tiger Woods, a newer, deeper understanding and appreciation for the game has emerged. Around the globe, an estimated 67 million people of different ages, genders, and backgrounds are playing golf on a regular basis. A round of golf is both physical and mental exercise that can be welcomed by most people.

The social aspect of golf is a significant feature of the game. It can be an excellent way of establishing new friendships and business connections. Players of different talents and proficiency levels can compete against each other on equal terms, thanks to a system of handicaps. On the individual level, one may be fighting the personal battle of lowering a handicap or striving to complete a round at par on the golfer's favorite course. A golf career can be a series of personal challenges with either a sense of frustration or a sense of achievement. Among those who have attempted to play the game of golf, it is obvious that anyone can play, but not everyone can play well. If a golfer aspires to be one of the few who do play well, s/he may wish to explore what physical and mental conditioning can do for his or her game.

Golf is unique in the arena of sports because it is as much, or more, a mental game as it is a physical one. A superficial look at a four and a half-hour golf game reveals isolated moments of action as players drive, chip, pitch, and putt, in an attempt to get a ball in one hole after another. Players spend much of the time, however, walking from hole to hole or simply standing in preparation for the next shot. This is not to say that the physical requirements of the golf game are trivial. How a player spends the inactive time on the golf course, however, may be just as important as the time he or she is actively involved in the game.

What happens in the psyche between and during shots is an essential part of the game. The physical activity is important, but so is the mental activity, or mental discipline, of the player. This discipline may or may not come naturally. If it does not come naturally, it can be learned for the benefit of the golfer's game. As will be seen in subsequent chapters, hatha yoga provides the ideal means of achieving the physical conditioning and mental discipline necessary for golf.

PHYSICAL CHALLENGES

From the physical perspective, what are the requirements in the game of golf? Many people do not think of golf as an athletic sport, requiring physical conditioning, but rather as a recreational activity, like a "walk in the park". Serious golfers, however, know that their physical condition affects the quality of play as much as their techniques and skills. Golf can, however, sometimes adversely affect a player's physiology. Golfers who are not well-conditioned and trained can experience fatigue, muscle soreness, or even injury.

What is the right age to play golf? Although some, like the famous Tiger Woods, begin the game while only a child, golf is a sport that is actually played more frequently by people as they get older. In fact, very often, many professional golfers do not reach their peak until they are in or past their mid-thirties. As players age, their physical conditioning becomes more important. An average player will cover five miles or more during each 18-hole round of golf. The intermittent nature of the walk on the golf course decreases the intensity of the workout, but for middle age and older individuals, such exercise can be of substantial benefit. Unfortunately, without proper preparation of the body, the exercise associated with golf may also be a health risk.

A golfing professional teaches the specific skills and techniques of the game, but the mechanics of golf must also be learned and committed to the individual's memory. Once proper instruction and practice time have been accomplished, the golfer must be able to recall the lessons while actively playing the game. A strong, flexible, and relaxed body is resistant to post-play fatigue. A well-conditioned body is less prone to possible injuries and performs better for the golfer.

There are several physical components to the game, and each requires different skills. Throughout the game, a golfer physically interacts with the equipment, clubs, ball, and golf course. A sense of relaxed connection and comfort with each element helps any golfer reach his/her full potential in playing the game. To carry out the mechanics of the game correctly, the golfer must learn how to perform each movement.

The golf grip is the most basic element in playing the game, followed by the grip in motion through the golf swing. The grip provides the golfer the vital contact with club and the club head with the ball. A good grip strikes a delicate balance between control and relaxation. A good grip on the club allows the player to begin in a neutral and balanced position and to follow through with a controlled and consistent swing. The position of the hands on the club determines the range of motion of the wrists, and the grip pressure dictates how freely, yet controlled, the arms and wrists move in the swing. The objective is to adopt a relaxed, but firm grip that results in just the right amount of control over the club head. Golfers try to control the movement (twisting) of the club head whether it is open or closed to achieve their desired ball flight.

The golf swing comprises the primary action in the game of golf. The swing is what golfers spend most of their time practicing. The best golfers have a smooth and consistent swing. The golf swing should be as simple as possible. It can be divided into grip, presentation to ball, back swing and down or through swing. As the golfers "play through" each round of golf, each of the steps of the golf swing must be executed in turn, smoothly without haste. Posture must be maintained throughout the stages, and focus must be on the coiling motion of the upper body as well as the movement of the feet.

To address the ball, one assumes the correct stance and posture, bringing the club head to the ball. To execute a more consistent and stronger golf swing, the stance is quite important. The stance should feel secure on the ground and well balanced. The golfer's weight should be evenly distributed between both feet, with the knees flexed.

Alignment is paramount with respect to the ball, the earth, and the target. Alignment of the golfer's body standing over the ball, and bringing the club to the address position, often determines how the swing will progress. The golfer's back should be kept straight, and the golfer's body should be neither crouched nor upright, as the club is brought to address the ball. Problems with posture may result in slices and/or hooks.

Power and distance in the golf swing comes from the coiling motion of the upper body, rather than from brute force. The motion of the swing begins with what is called a one-piece take away. Golfers find their key move i.e. solid hands, arm movement, shoulders etc. This should all be done with trying to keep the lower body stable. A recommended sequence of the wind up or back swing is hands, arms, shoulders, waist, legs and with some golfers, feet. Strength and flexibility in the torso, as well as shoulders and legs, all provide for powerful and accurate follow through. The scapular muscles of the upper back and the rotator cuff muscles of the shoulders need to be strong and well toned. Wrists, forearms, and shoulders need conditioning to withstand repeated impact with the ball. Strong elastic muscles from head to toe and fluid movements in all body parts improve rotation. Less effort is required and more power is yielded when the body is well positioned and conditioned.

The back swing is a turning and winding up motion in getting the golf club prepared for the golfer's down or through swing.

The downswing is where the uncoiling or release of the body/golf club is performed. The golfers must understand how the golf club should be released (swing action), then try to use as many parts of their body as possible to do it with more power and complete balance.

The follow-through is that part of the swing during and after impact with the ball. The body uncoils fully with the right hip (or the left hip for a left-hander) and shoulder pointing at the ball's original position, and the body facing down the target line. The arms follow through to bring the club head around the back of the head. The important part of the follow-through is that the club head is released with the ball down the target line. When the club head is in contact with the ball, it must move along the target line.

The short game in golf includes the components of pitching, chipping, and putting the ball. The short chipping and pitching strokes incorporate the same fundamentals as the full swing. The movement of the body, the angle of the clubface, as well as the position of the club head, hands, and body through the hitting area are all similar, if not identical, to what one might consider in the full swing. Some say that the grip is a little tighter in the chip. The chip and the pitch are both just smaller swings.

Once the golfer has managed to get the ball onto the green, the putting begins. Putting properly has some physical requirements subtly different from the golf swing. The relaxation of certain body parts is as critical as a sense of aim and the force on the ball. The putt is all about pivoting the upper body around the head. The swing is like a pendulum, smooth and rhythmic. Some consider putting to be an art form rather than a science. Because there is more finesse in these shots, there can be a tendency for players to over-think each shot, spending too much time trying to make sure all factors of an attempt have been addressed. Trying too hard, however, can inhibit the golfer's instincts on the green.

While bringing the club to the ball with a smooth stroke, the player should maintain a posture that is relaxed and at ease. The upper body does most of the work, with the arms, hands, and club following. The majority of the body, the lower body and the head, must be kept still and stress-free, but not stooped. When putting, it is important to resist the urge to look up as this can cause the swing plane to alter, thus pushing the ball off the target line.

The green is as much an instrument of play as the putter itself, and the ability to read greens is as important as the putting technique. Greens are usually sloped, making the mind's eye an important instrument in the game. One needs to know what line the ball should take, how hard to strike it, and how to judge speed. The grain of the green will affect the speed and direction of the putt. Above all, the golfer must maintain a positive mental attitude.

Stretching and strengthening not only improves the grip, stance, and swings, but calls for a commitment to fitness which can help golfers establish the endurance to carry their golf bags and clubs for 18 holes. Most importantly physical fitness also, helps golfers prevent golf injuries. (A leading cause of injuries among golfers is a lack of physical conditioning.) Sadly, some players believe that injuries are just another part of the game. Many older professionals attempt to play through their injuries and stop playing only when absolutely necessary.

A look at the most common injuries gives an even clearer indication of where physical strength and flexibility are required in the game of golf. Several factors contribute to the strains or pulls of the muscles, tendons, and ligaments in the lower back. Strains represent the most common type of injury among golfers. The severe twisting motion of a golf swing, insufficient warm-ups, poor flexibility and lack of overall physical condition are all contributing factors to golf injuries. Lower back pain can result from a lack of flexibility in the hamstrings. The hamstrings attach to the pelvis. If the hamstrings are tight, they can negatively affect the lower back. Strengthening abdominal muscles, which support the lower back, can help to prevent pain. If these muscles are weak, one might lean over too much in the golf posture and put undue strain on the back.

The arms, the wrists and the elbow joints are particularly susceptible to injuries. Problems in the arms include tendonitis in the lateral elbow. Golf injuries to the outside elbow typically occur on the left arm for right-handed golfers, as golfers pull in the golf swing, stretching the tendons in the lateral elbow.

Excessive grip pressure places additional stress on the tendons. Right elbow injuries can take the form of strains or tears to the small ligament that connects the two bones on the medial elbow. This ligament damage can be caused by a weak grip or excessive rotation of the forearms during the downswing. (Some rotation is normal.) Over-rotation accentuates the load on the inside of the elbow and increases the risk of injury there.

Golfers may suffer from hitting too many balls, from the trauma of striking the ground or from hitting the ball incorrectly. Such hitting has an adverse effect on the wrists, since the shock of the impact travels up, through the wrist first, followed by the rest of the arm, the elbow, and the shoulder.

The complicated structure of the shoulder is also vulnerable when golfing. Four muscles and their tendons come together in the region of the shoulder, called the rotator cuff. Much attention is given to the rotator cuff because several injuries, such as bursitis, tendonitis, and tears, are possible in this area.

As golfers bring back their arms for a golf swing, they may get pinching of the bursa, the part of the joint with fluid that lubricates the joint. Inflammation to the joint begins as bursitis, which can progress to tendonitis, then to an actual tear. A tear is more likely to occur in the shoulder, which is under more stress in the swing. There are several expectations or requirements of the rotator cuff and other muscles of the shoulder. They must allow the arm to rotate back in the swing, stop it from going too far, then get it going forward again.

Although acute injuries (such as fractures and sprains from a single swing or blow) can happen in the game of golf, most injuries are caused by the cumulative effect of incorrect body mechanics and/or repeated impact with the ball or ground. Increasing muscle strength and flexibility around all body joints reduces the likelihood of injury, allowing them to move with strength and to absorb some impact of the play.

Even without actual injury, the game of golf can still negatively affect the body, if played improperly. Without proper preparation, the golfer, especially the occasional enthusiast, may experience fatigue during and especially after the game. Muscles can become sore from using them in a manner for which they are not conditioned, thereby reducing enjoyment of the game. No one wants to endure any suffering as a result of a recreational activity.

All these elements of the physical game revolve around some common themes. The importance of <u>flexibility and strength</u> are evident in stance and swing. <u>Balance</u> is crucial, also. The <u>ability to relax</u> those body parts that are not being used in the immediate action helps the golfer execute swings with ease, especially while putting. Yoga addresses each of these aspects of the game. Yoga develops all of them through practice, and results in better play. Yoga techniques improve the game of golf.

MENTAL CHALLENGES

Once the physical conditioning issues are addressed and the techniques of the game, such as the golf swing and the putt, are committed to the subconscious mind, the psychology of the game needs attention. Without a technique for <u>mastering the psyche</u> in the game of golf, players may remain frustrated, stressed and disappointed with their performance. We are all at the mercy of mind and emotions. The psychological game --- including attitude, relaxation abilities, visual skills and emotional control --- plays a vital role in golfing success. Too much anxiety in play can lead to physical tension, and physical tension can kill the golf swing.

Golf can be a competitive game whether one is playing against oneself or others. Self-destructive thoughts can impinge on the game of the best players. During the game, golfers psychologically interact with the equipment, the golf course, co-players, spectators and themselves.

Common mental "traps" include anxiety or nervousness on the course, loss of focus, and the inability to separate oneself emotionally from the progress of the game. Golfers suffer when any of these factors goes out of control. When golfers worry excessively, become upset or angry over the game, become overly pleased with their performance, or let the play or sportsmanship of others affect their own mental state, erratic play can result.

The mechanics and logistics of the game make golf a difficult game to master. They are often in conflict with what the mind and body want to do, especially when the golfer is under pressure.

The adrenaline rush or excitement of the game has no easy outlet. Athletes in other sports, such as football, hockey or basketball, can diffuse or adapt their urge of "fight or flight" more readily through the action of the game. Running and bodily contact can help alleviate the physical manifestations of stress in the game. In golf, the time spent poised over the ball or walking the course can too easily be spent thinking and worrying. Excess energy and anxiety can build with no release.

Fear is at the root of most golfer perceived threats that trigger a mind-body defense mechanism. This mechanism is often termed the "fight or flight" response. Physical manifestations of this reaction are the body sending overloads of adrenaline, dopamine and other hormones through the nervous system in preparation for some physical action. Too much adrenaline pumped through the body results in tension and doubt.

Fear defense systems vary individually. Some people are naturally more calm and relaxed under pressure and don't let problems or frustration get to them. Others are more sensitive to stress and may become upset much more easily. One might think that golfers experience a limited need to respond to fear during a simple game of golf, yet sources of fear are varied during the game. Fear can come from anxiety about self-esteem and what others think about the player. Fear may also be imbedded in topping the ball. Fear of fear itself is natural, too.

"Will I hit the ball?" "Will the ball go where I want it to go?" "Will others play well?" "Will the others think that I am playing well?" "Will I lose my temper and become angry or upset over my play or the play of others?" Anxiety is largely an attempt to defend pride or ego. Most often, golfers are not aware of their ego, or do not admit their pride, so they are not able to develop a strategy for reducing such anxiety.

Fear feels uncomfortable, largely because we have not learned how to deal with it. Most humans, by nature, don't like the feelings evoked by confrontations with others or even themselves, but unless golfers get used to such feelings, consistently good performance under pressure remains highly unlikely.

For instance, as the golfer simply stands over a ball, the arms and body might start to do unusual or uncontrolled things, creating such uncomfortable feelings, called "choking." There are numerous types of chokes --- tensing up and gripping the club too tightly, playing too fast, coming up short with putts or even just trying too hard.

Emotions can interfere with mind-body unity, breathing and concentration, spoiling the tempo of the swing, decision-making, confidence and, worst of all, enjoyment of the game. Most often, compromising feelings come from too much thinking and worrying about what others may think. Hitting a bad shot at a crucial time can stay in the golfer's memory for years.

When fearing a long drive or missing a short putt to win a match, increased adrenaline, heart rate, blood pressure and respiration prepare the body to deal with a threat by increasing anxiety. While never really in physical danger, the golfer suffers anxiety triggered by a perception of a threat to self-esteem or ego. When the fear defense system kicks in, the golfer becomes agitated. Whether feeling more powerful or less able, the golfer is usually vulnerable. The energy of fear becomes self-destructive, resulting in tension, lack of confidence and poor shots. To fully enjoy the game of golf, it is important to understand the mind-body defense system of fear. As long as scores are kept in mental or written form, golfers have expectations. When cards are compared during or after the game, ego comes into play with the sport of golf. Being aware of the physiological way that the body works can be the most important part of the game. Accomplished golfers can change their mind-body chemistry simply by changing their thinking --- from fear and tension to more positive emotions, such as joy.

FOCUS

Many fears can contribute to a lack of focus during the game. Fears comprise the mental portions of the distractions, but there are also physical distractions. *Yoga techniques make it possible to quiet the mind and focus on the task at hand.*

Golf has perhaps more potential physical distractions than any other sport -- trees, rough, water hazards, bunkers, opponents, score, weather, and wind. Knowing the lay of the land is helpful in the physical aspect of the game. What does the hole look like? Where are the ponds, the rough, or the trees?

Many golfers, both professional and amateur, suffer from a condition known as "rabbit ears." They are overly sensitive to everything that is occurring around them on the course. Each noise or movement in the periphery of the game causes great aggravation, and the golfer must also cope with the added distraction of spectators. The traditional etiquette and decorum long associated with the game of golf at all levels have always dictated that there must be silence and stillness when a player is executing a shot. Such a hush is something that players have come to expect.

Whether professional or amateur, why are some players more prone to distraction than others? Some believe that coping strategies are the result of mental focus or mental fatigue.

As in most other areas of life, success in golf is often measured not by how one performs, but how one reacts when obstacles get in the way. Positive thinking and relaxation with a cleansing breath after a wayward shot can produce a burst of fresh oxygen, with released muscular tension. After a cleansing breath, at least for a brief moment, the rest of the game seems more manageable. Good golfers don't dwell on bad shots. Good golfers let their mind do its job and let the rest of the body relax, as they minimize the effects of too much thinking. Being attached to the outcome of a game can manifest itself in the loss of temper over a bad shot, when the golfer becomes angry and frustrated. It is important to learn how to play from hole to hole without projecting the outcome and without dwelling on past shots. Keeping perspective in the game, maintaining a relaxed mental attitude, and cultivating positive thinking are goals that all golfers should try to attain.

In the following chapters we will look at the practice of hatha yoga and how yoga ideally addresses each of the physical and mental challenges that are involved in playing the game of golf. One's ability to benefit from yoga through focus on alignment, strength, balance, and flexibility is tremendous. The mind-body emphasis in yoga allows the golfer to acquire the mental discipline needed for relaxed, healthy, and enjoyable play. Through yoga, casual golfers and professionals alike can improve their physical condition and develop internal skills to improve their game. All golfers can learn to calm down with deep breathing and lessen their anxious feelings before pre-round or pre-shot routines. Golf is a game that can be improved, but not necessarily perfected. The practice of yoga develops acceptance of non-perfection and comfort with the golfer's daily level of play.

CHAPTER 3: YOGA BRINGS PEACE TO GOLF

For several thousands of years, Yoga has traditionally been used as a path to enlightenment. Yoga has been the path to our true nature and pure consciousness. When one's true nature is realized, there is nothing else to acquire – a genuine perspective is attained. Yoga is not a religion, but it is one of several orthodox systems of Indian philosophy. Its simple precepts were originally handed down generation to generation, orally from teacher to student. With the advent of writing, the philosophy of Yoga was outlined in depth in *The Yoga Sutras* of Patanjali and the *Hatha Yoga Pradipika*.

The Yoga Sutras outline the eightfold path or astanga, eight branches of yoga. The branches are guidelines for living life with awareness and responsibility for one's actions. They include principles of moral and ethical conduct, self-discipline, health and spiritual focus.

The essence of this book is that branch of yoga called hatha yoga. It focuses on the physical aspects of yoga and preparation for meditation, specifically preparing the body and mind for stillness. In a broader sense, hatha yoga is a science of living.

Yoga is practiced around the world today for many reasons. On one level, yoga is beneficial for maintaining or regaining physical health. It is also a means for balancing the nervous system, calming a busy mind, and living in a more conscious and purposeful manner. Regular practice of yoga can result in physical and emotional strength and stability. It is a discipline that increases awareness and control over the interplay of strength, flexibility, coordination, and endurance. Yoga is a natural stress reducer with cardio-vascular and psychological benefits. Like the game of golf, more people tend to practice yoga as they get older. Yoga emphasizes thoughtful conditioning of the body. It attracts people who do not want to wear out their bodies, but rather to make them more vibrant.

Hatha yoga is primarily concerned with the two branches of yoga called asana and pranayama. The term asana has come to mean pose or position, although it originally referred to the seat of the yogi in meditation. Each asana is an opportunity for the practitioner to gain strength, flexibility, and balance, all while maintaining a sense of calm peace. The asanas can be done standing, sitting, or lying down. Asanas focus on the spine as the foundation of the body. Many yoga movements involve bending forward, backward, and sideways as well as twisting, all of which promote strength and flexibility of the spine. These movements also stimulate the spinal nerves, affecting other areas of the body. The practice of yoga addresses the entire musculo-skeletal system. Attention is paid, also, to the internal systems of the body, including the nervous, respiratory, circulatory, digestive, and endocrine systems. Specific asanas will influence the function of each system.

The other major branch of hatha yoga is pranayama. The word pranayama means, "to embody or house the life force energy", "breath extension" or "breath control". It is a category of special breathing techniques that are used to enhance the practice of the asanas, and pranayama is also a practice unto itself. The term prana not only means "breath" but can also refer to "energy, life, or vitality." With this in mind, the scope of the practice expands to include an increase in vital life force energy. Yoga emphasizes deep diaphragmatic breathing. Complete breathing improves the functioning of the lungs and provides a means of nourishing the entire body with oxygen, while removing carbon dioxide and other wastes. Poor oxygenation can result in a decrease in concentration and mental clarity, with the result of increased mental fatigue.

The benefits of the pranayama are numerous. The practice of breath awareness improves respiratory function and increases oxygen throughout the entire body. Breathing fully encourages proper alignment of the spine and therefore, improves posture. Full breathing also engages the muscles of the torso, thus improving their tone. By concentrating on different phases of breathing, one can achieve serious results. Focusing on inhalation produces a stimulating, energizing effect. Focusing on exhalation results in more relaxation.

Hatha Yoga is also a method of self-healing and wellness that systematically dissolves stress and increases awareness of the self. In yoga the practitioner becomes whole as the breath is synchronized with movement and restful alertness. This style of movement is a contemplative form of exercise that stresses self-pacing and patience.

With the practice of yoga one becomes immersed in the process and avoids self-distraction. (One is not encouraged to watch TV during the practice of yoga.) In the practice of hatha yoga, the depth of integration between the breath and the physical movement of breathing accents the importance of the mind-body connection. This focus sets yoga apart from other programs of physical conditioning. It integrates the whole body, involving all of its systems --- structural, glandular, and energetic. Yoga is a practice of mental and physical conditioning with an inward focus that cultivates self-awareness and clarity. The mind has an obvious role in any physical movement, but yoga practice coordinates and deepens the involvement. By working at a slower pace, concentrating on the quality of movement, one can focus on listening to the body and any emotions that may arise.

Yoga is not competitive or goal-oriented. The only goal of yoga is to participate fully in the actual practice itself. In yoga one gains a deeper knowledge of the physical self and awareness of the body's movement. One's mental focus is on the moment-to-moment unfolding of physical movement and eventually of life itself. Students of yoga may become so present in the moment that they develop an objectivity or experience of the silent witness during the practice. The process (in practice, golf, and life) is most important.

Yoga can be seen as a metaphor for life. As one works through the practice, one continues to breathe and to explore sensations on a moment-by-moment basis. The internal focus can result in greater self-confidence and inner peace. Yoga practice awakens energy in the body and, at the same time, trains the mind to become more quiet, yet more creative and dynamic. Out of this deep relaxation comes greater energy and clarity. An inner balance is created between alertness and activity. When working through the poses of hatha yoga, practitioners often encounter many emotions --- especially anxiety, anger, fear, and vulnerability. Moving, living and breathing through yoga are a practice for living life itself.

Chapter 4: The Benefits of Yoga for the Physical Game of Golf

Hatha yoga is a unique science of mental and physical conditioning. Its benefits go beyond the physical, harmonizing the mind and the body. Such harmony is an essential quality for success in any activity, especially sports. Yoga enhances flexibility, strength, balance and alignment of the body. It creates a free flow of energy through the body and restores the body to a healthier and more natural state. Yoga relaxes and opens the body as well as the mind. All of these qualities are vital in the game of golf. As yoga develops each of these qualities, the golfer enjoys improved performance on the golf course with a reduced chance of injury. In short, the golfer attains greater enjoyment of the game.

FLEXIBILITY

Golf requires that the body be "warmed-up" and flexible for several reasons. Warming-up prepares one for a round of golf, but a simple warm-up before the game does not produce the same lasting benefits as consistent conditioning of the body through the practice of yoga. Most sports and exercises lead to the shortening and contracting of certain muscles. Exercise for other sports frequently concentrates on a small number of muscles, which leaves stiffness in the rest of the body.

Yoga, on the other hand, involves slow and conscious stretching and contracting of all of the muscles, tendons and ligaments. Yoga practice promotes greater muscle tone. Since longer muscles work more efficiently than shorter ones, yoga improves the body's performance. The methods of movement and stretching in yoga also relieve tensions that are stored in the cells of the muscles. The increased physical flexibility resulting from such a program expands one's range of motion in all phases of the golf game. As one addresses the ball, whether it is in preparation for a drive or a putt, the golfer must be flexible. The golfer needs flexibility in the legs and lower back to attain the ideal posture for addressing the ball. If the golfer's stance is too upright, slicing or hooking may occur.

A great deal of flexibility is required at all stages in the swing. Flexibility allows the golfer to rotate further in the swing and, therefore, hit the ball farther. The legs, knees, hamstrings, and hips in the first stage of the swing, all need to be supple to prevent injury. The golfer must prevent him/herself from the possibility of pulling/tearing muscles, ligaments, and tendons. Tightness in the hamstrings can affect the lower back, since the hamstrings attach to the pelvis. The ability to move the torso in a wide range of motion is also essential. Reduced strain on the body is directly related to the power of the resultant swing. For the swing to be fluid and smooth, the golfer must have a supple back, spine, side-body and abdominal muscles. Ideally, the spine needs flexibility in the lateral directions.

The golfer also needs significant mobility in the arm and shoulder regions. Successful swinging requires that the golfer be able to raise the club to a specific height and follow through with strength and fluidity. A free flow of energy in the body allows for optimal performance.

STRENGTH

Flexible muscles must also be strong for golfers to attain top performance. The upper body is a key area for a strong golf swing. Increasing muscle strength around the joints, shoulders, elbows, and wrists will reduce the likelihood of injury in these areas. Building up muscles in the shoulders is especially important. Strong forearms and shoulder muscles can help reduce the risk of injury and help absorb some of the shock from the impact of repeatedly hitting the ball, accidentally hitting the ground, or hitting the ball incorrectly. Strong abdominal and back muscles prevent lower back stress that can occur as a result of trying to maintain a correct posture through the swing. Because the pelvis and hips initiate the swing rotation, the golfer must have the strength to prevent back strain, especially in these lower regions.

Yoga practice improves strength and endurance, by working all muscle groups of the body. Rather than using external weights, yoga uses the weight of the body to strengthen itself. The dynamic flow of some asanas increases cardio-vascular strength, endurance and stamina. Asanas create power through the systematic contraction and relaxation of body muscles. Tension in muscles that are not involved in the immediate activity can consume power and energy. Conscious movements of only those regions of the body that are needed at any given moment, however, allow for more efficient use of strength. Learning to strengthen different parts of the body helps the golfer to economize energy by using only the appropriate muscles during activity.

ALIGNMENT

Every asana in the practice of yoga has specific points of alignment for the body. Correctly positioning the body produces physical awareness. Alignment in golf can refer to several things. Body alignment is important for properly playing golf as well as many other sports. Misalignment during practice or the game, itself, can lead to imbalances in the body and possible injury. In all stages of the game, golf requires a sense of alignment and attention to posture. The position and angle of the spine must be maintained from the address through the backward coil of the swing. Alignment of the body throughout the game mirrors the level of the golfer's skill and determines quality of play.

The golfer must pay attention to alignment of the ball and the target, to bring the two together. Moving the ball through the course, step by step, the player repeatedly focuses on direction and angle. In the putting phase of the game, the contours of the earth come into the picture, and the golfer needs to account for and use this information, too. Alignment of the putt requires adjustment to get the ball to the target.

BALANCE

Balance in the movements of the game and in the body is another challenge for the golfer. Yoga allows for the correction of imbalances by working both sides of the body. Consistent practice of yoga, with its emphasis on alignment, can prevent muscle imbalance and weakness in less used muscle groups. Opening the energy channels, with balanced attention to both sides of the body, creates improved health. As the golfer interacts with the earth in several stages of the golf game, the concept of balance and grounding is important. In the golf swing, from address to follow through, the golfer needs to maintain balance in relation to the ground. As the golfer shifts his/her weight from one foot to the other in the process of swinging, steadiness improves performance. The golfer's weight must be distributed about fifty-fifty, from right foot to left foot and also fifty-fifty from the balls of the feet to the heels. Better players continue to move and adjust their foot position until they establish a balanced position.

Balance within the golfer's body is also important, especially as golfers swing from one side of the body, with an inherent asymmetry in the use of the body. Muscles on one side of the body may become tighter, more developed and therefore overtaxed. The underutilized muscle groups can result in a less flexible, weaker side. Balance is desirable because a golf swing that is symmetrical in strength will be more accurate and powerful.

Another benefit of yoga practice is balance in breathing, harmonizing and integrating the breath with the body. A proper deep, diaphragmatic breath moves the belly, filling it and gently massaging the internal organs. The yoga-conditioned golfer can use breathing to open and lengthen muscles, to cleanse away physical toxins, and to release emotional tensions. Proper breathing increases circulation and cardiovascular capacity. Breath is also a natural stress reducer. The heartbeat slows naturally as the diaphragm stimulates the vagus nerve. Steady breathing through obstacles improves the golfer's performance.

The fluid movements of yoga can ensure the free flow of energy in the body. Energy can move to those areas of the body that need it at any particular phase of the game.

Each of the physical benefits of yoga outlined here not only affect the quality of play and help to prevent injuries, but each can also help a golfer recover more quickly after a game. Strong, flexible muscles are less likely to be sore after play. Efficient use of the muscles results in action that is focused with a body that is relaxed. The golfer who practices hatha yoga has greater energy and vitality at the end of the game to further enjoy the experience.

Chapter 5: Benefits of Yoga for the Mentality and Psychology of Golf

Practicing the mechanics of the game of golf and physical conditioning alone still are not enough to ensure the golfer's success on the fairway. Just as important as the physical requirements of the game are the psychological challenges. One can practice the swing and play golf a million times, yet still fail to hit that successful shot when under pressure. Relaxation and mental focus may or may not come with additional practice and experience on the course. The other element to successful play, mental discipline, therefore must also be learned.

Yoga, a mind-body method of exercise, addresses the mental and psychological aspect of the game as well as the physical. The poses of yoga are not only a physical activity, but they are also a mental and psychological discipline. When successful golfers work through a pose, they focus on what they are feeling and how they are moving. By making subtle adjustments, golfers can make their poses feel even better through the process of mental and psychological awareness. Yoga is a practice that is perfect cross training for golf.

The brain responds better to direct, proactive orders. Positive thinking takes practice and the advised practice of yoga can help you, as a golfer, to achieve a better inner attitude. With the practice of yoga, you are about to learn techniques that bring your attention inward, working the game moment-by-moment, concentrating on the processes of the body and the game.

The very practice of yoga teaches the golfer how to move in the present. In the practice, each asana is performed step by step, with focus on the body and the breath. Physical awareness is emphasized along with the mental state of being present with movements and feelings. The mind is quieted and the moment comes alive when the golfer can synchronize and balance the breath and the movements of play. The slow, conscious practice of yoga trains golfers to bring their mind to the present, dissolving projections and expectations. Such yoga practice provides more benefits than any program of physical conditioning alone.

One of the essential sutras from the *Yoga Sutras of Patanjali* translates to, "The restraint of the modification of the mind-stuff is Yoga." Yoga teaches the practitioners to become aware of their thought patterns and mental habits. Golfers do not have to be victims of their own thoughts. Thoughts can be changed or quieted altogether through yoga.

When the inner chatter begins on the golf course, the golfer should acknowledge it for what it is, then let it go. Thoughts and questions like, "What if I miss the ball altogether?" and "Will everyone laugh at me if my shot is bad?" are counter-productive.

Focusing the mind on the body and on breath awareness can help increase the golfer's concentration and centering during play. Mental focus serves to eliminate the "noise", both internal and external, that can prevent the golfer from achieving the best game. Instead of thinking: "I have to hit this shot just right," the yoga-trained golfer can teach the mind to be still.

Now, as you begin to learn how yoga can help you improve your game of golf, the mental practice of yoga can make your game more enjoyable, too.

NOTES

PART TWO

CHAPTER 6: GOLFER'S YOGA PROGRAM

The program outlined here is a sport-specific yoga program designed for golfers who wish to improve their golf game, but non-golfers can use the program as well. You do not have to be flexible to practice yoga. You do not have to be strong to practice yoga. The promised benefit of yoga is to become physically stronger and more flexible with practice. Yoga also yields more mental concentration and self-confidence. Regular practice will help to train the mind and prepare the body, committing the physical and mental aspects of the program to the subconscious.

As you begin to apply on the golf course yoga learned from this book, remember that yoga is not a means to achieve an external goal. Instead, through the practice of yoga, you concentrate on becoming more aware of what is right at any given moment, and you also derive more enjoyment from the very process itself, as it unfolds. Yoga allows for a unique relaxed mind as you do not compete with yourself or others. Yoga practitioners must remember that what you accomplish today may not be possible tomorrow. Each day, each practice session, and each game is a new beginning.

Yoga should feel good. If you are feeling what you perceive to be extreme pain, you need to adjust your posture or come out of it altogether. During yoga, your breath gives you immediate feedback. If your breath becomes labored or stops altogether, it may be a sign that you are over-doing it. Forcing yourself through pain can actually prevent you from relaxing and stretching. Ignoring pain can result in injury. Your muscles tense and tighten in response to fear and extreme discomfort. Because pain is relative, with yoga you move into a higher threshold of practice that "hurts so good."

Now you can begin to find the missing peace through yoga. You should be both relaxed and alert as you perform the asanas. Bring your awareness inward. Keep your attention focused on maintaining your breath and observing how your body feels. Your breath should be smooth and even. Breathe in and out through the nose, as breathing is designed to prepare the air for the lungs. Breathing brings the essential life force energy to every cell of your body. Breathing warms or cools the air, and moisturizes it, removing any dust or debris. Remember that your lungs are large, and they are intended to be used completely top to bottom, front to back.

A special breathing practice, or pranayama, is called *Ujjayi* breathing, or victorious breath. Ujjayi breath should be utilized throughout the entire yoga asana portions of the practice session. This type of breathing helps you to concentrate and become calm while building heat, endurance, and stamina. By increasing the time it takes to inhale and exhale, you develop breath control and expand your lung capacity. A longer breath slows the heartbeat and reduces stress.

Ujjayi breathing is performed by breathing in and out through the nose while slightly constricting the glottis in the throat, the opening between the vocal cords. The result is an audible breath with a soft, snore-like sound. Some think of it as an ocean-like sound, flowing in and out. If you stop breathing or breathing becomes difficult or labored, you can decide if you are pushing yourself beyond your limits.

The quality of breath is a key sign in determining the difference between intensity of movement and pain, between fatigue and lethargy. Your breath should be effortless, steady and smooth. In every moment your breath is a reflection of your state of mind and emotions. By becoming aware of your breathing and introducing different patterns of breathing, you can begin to determine your state of being, both mentally and physically.

Where and when you practice is your individual decision. You can practice yoga almost anytime and anywhere, but you will get the most out of it if you are not distracted during practice. Some people prefer to practice in the morning, others in the afternoon or evening.

One of the benefits of yoga as physical and mental conditioning is that the poses can be adapted in numerous ways to fit the needs of each person. Slight changes and modifications can make the program possible for everyone. Everyone has individual strengths and weaknesses. You can choose not to do a particular asana or sequence if it does not feel right to you, or you can modify it. Listen to your body and move into each pose slowly. Do not push yourself beyond your edge to the point of pain. Just approach the edge.

The rest of this program is divided into three distinct sections. The *first section* is the warm-up portion of the program. It consists of seven exercises. Each, including the first pranayama exercise as breathing technique, was chosen to prepare the body for asana practice. The *second section* consists of eleven yoga asanas, or poses, including a posture flow sequence called the sun salutation. They are the essence of the program, selected for their benefits in conditioning for golf. Integration, that allows the relaxation and recovery of the body after practice, is the *final section* of the program. The entire practice program should take you about 45 minutes.

<u>*When and how often should you practice?*</u> No specific time is prescribed to start practice. It is not necessary to practice yoga just prior to your golf game, but practice at that time won't hurt. The forty-five minutes of exercises can be done at any time during the day.

For maximum benefit you should practice the yoga program once each day. Daily practice not only improves your game of golf, but also brings contentment, enjoyment and purpose for all aspects of your life. It is recommended that the program be practiced at least three times a week, more if possible. You should make it a point to do the 9-minute warm-up before your game.

The benefit derived varies from person to person; nevertheless, the following guidelines should be kept in mind:

See how much You can benefit !

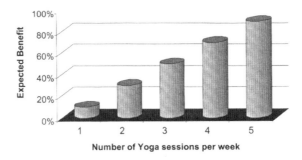

Expected Benefit

Number of Yoga sessions per week

Each exercise or asana section includes:
- An introduction to and explanation of the exercise or pose, and how its practice specifically applies to the improvement of your golf game.
- A description of how to perform the exercise or pose and how you should come into and out of the pose, as well as how to breathe during the pose.
- The number and duration of repetitions to perform and for how long you should hold the pose (number of breaths).

Under certain circumstances it may be appropriate for individual sections of the program to be used as stand-alone practice. For instance, the warm-up section consists of exercises that can be used before actually playing a round of golf. Preparing the body for play can be especially helpful in the prevention of injuries. Muscles that are warm and stretched before tee time are more able to fulfill their highest potential. The breathing techniques would be appropriate throughout the game for calming the mind and body during difficult moments of play.

If you have recently undergone surgery or have any serious physical illness or disease, check with your physician before beginning this practice. Under certain circumstances and conditions, particular postures and techniques should be performed with great care and awareness, or avoided altogether.

Check the list of contraindications below before doing the asanas:

Condition	Sciatica
Avoid	Forward bends or intense stretching of hamstrings
Condition	Menstruation
Avoid	Inverted Poses, strenuous abdominal poses
Condition	Hypertension/ High Blood Pressure
Avoid	Inverted poses, bellows breath
Condition	Glaucoma, other eye problems, and ear congestion
Avoid	Inverted poses
Condition	Pregnancy
Avoid	Inverted poses, belly down poses

NOTE: Illustrations that follow indicate the correct asanas. Photographs are included as examples.

It is important to move slowly and consciously during yoga practice, taking personal responsibility for your safety. Listen to your body, recognize when something does not feel right to you. Make the necessary adjustments and modifications. Practice compassion for yourself and peaceful acceptance of your body as it is right now. Remember that everything changes. With time and patience positive changes will occur.

Yoga Basic Dos and Don'ts

DOs:
• **Do** allow adequate time after eating to begin your practice.
• **Do** find a quiet area to practice. Turn off your phones and pagers.
• **Do** eliminate distractions while you are practicing.
• **Do** take time away from worldly activities to focus inwardly.
• **Do** remember that everything changes.
• **Do** breathe deeply. Let the breath deepen the pose for you.
• **Do** open a window for fresh air during breathing practices, or do your practice outside in nice weather.
• **Do** be sensitive to your "edge" in each pose - that place where you can sustain holding the posture with deep breath and steadiness.
• **Do** move into sensations with patience, compassion, and awareness. (Your edge may change during the practice and in between practice sessions.)
• **Do** strike a balance between comfort and discomfort in the poses.
• **Do** listen to your breath for feedback.
• **Do** notice all thoughts and feelings during your practice.
• **Do** keep gently bringing your mind back to your practice if you find your mind wandering or distracted.

DON'Ts:
• **Don't** watch TV or read while doing yoga.
• **Don't** eat while practicing.
• **Don't** force yourself into a pose.
• **Don't** worry too much about doing the exercises perfectly in the beginning.
• **Don't** be over-critical of yourself.
• **Don't** rush through the practice.
• **Don't** practice on slippery or uneven surfaces.
• **Don't** hold your breath during the poses.
• **Don't** compare yourself to others.

ACCESSORIES

Yoga requires no equipment, but the following accessories can make the practice of yoga safer and more enjoyable.

1. Sticky Mat: Do not slip while practicing your postures. This foam, sticky mat offers a comfortable gripping surface, necessary for safe and effective yoga practice. This mat easily rolls up for portability and storage. Generally the sticky mat size is 68" to 72" long x 24" wide and approximately 1/8" thick. It is available in a variety of colors.

2. Blocks: Bring the ground to you. Initially if you are unable to reach the floor, a set of yoga blocks can help you achieve and maintain proper positioning. Made of lightweight foam, 4" x 6" x 9" blocks, weigh about 5 oz. each. Matching colors are available.

3. Yoga strap: Some of the asanas require that you extend your arms' reach. A strap of soft cotton webbing, 6' long 1" wide, can make stretching more comfortable. Straps are available in a variety of colors.

4. Eye pillow: Let your eyes relax. This soft silk pillow instantly helps you close your eyes and relax during corpse pose and meditation while lying down. Made of cool, soft silk filled with flax seed and herbs, this eye pillow can help to relax your eyes and sooth away tension.

5. A carry all bag is a convenient way to keep your accessories organized.

6. Tissues, if desired.

Log on to:
www.themissingpeace.net
or
www.barbed-wire.net/purple/TheMissingPeaceGolf.html
to obtain more information and order any accessories for your personal need.

ACCESSORIES

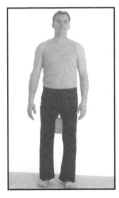
With Block

With Belt

With Belt

With Blocks

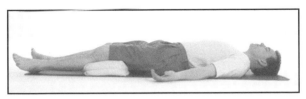
With Cushion

With Cushion & Eyepillow

CHAPTER 7: WARM UPS

It is important to realize that stretching and warming-up are not the same things. You cannot stretch to warm-up, but you must warm-up to stretch. Attempting to stretch cold or cool muscles is ineffective and an invitation to injury. The warm-up portion of any program of physical conditioning is essential. Warm-up increases the elasticity of the muscles, which reduces the likelihood of injury. Stretching and strengthening of muscles prior to yoga increases the effectiveness of the practice. Warm-ups increase circulation and energy flow to the muscles and joints.

The following set of opening exercises prepares the body for the asanas. They allow for an increasing flow of heat to the major muscle groups of the arms, legs, and torso. Remember that using this portion of the program before beginning a round of golf can be very helpful.

YOGA EXERCISES

Section	No.	Technique	Duration Minutes	Cumulative Time
Warm-up (7)	**1**	**Mountain Pose**	**1:00**	**1**
	2	**Swinging with Ha**	**2:00**	**3**
	3	**Spinning**	**1:00**	**4**
	4	**Wood Chopper**	**1:00**	**5**
	5	**Chair Pose**	**1:00**	**6**
	6	**Upward / Downward Facing Dog**	**2:00**	**8**
	7	**Bellows Breath**	**1:00**	**9**
Asanas (11)	8	Revolving Triangle	1:00	10
	9	Standing Yoga Mudra	1:00	11
	10	Tree Pose	2:00	13
	11	Spinal Twist and Hold	2:00	15
	12	Cobbler's Stretch	2:00	17
	13	Pigeon Stretch	2:00	19
	14	Snake Pose	2:00	21
	15	Sitting Still **MID-POINT**	3:00	24
	16	Sun Salutations	10:00	34
	17	Eye Exercise	1:00	35
	18	Neck Rolls	2:00	37
Integration (3)	19	Alternative Nostril Breathing	2:00	39
	20	Three Stage Breathing	2:00	41
	21	Corpse Pose	4:00	45

To begin your conditioning for golf, begin with a nine-minute

WARM-UP using the seven exercises that follow:

1. MOUNTAIN POSE

Mountain Pose is a very basic yoga pose that is the foundation for many other asanas. It brings your focus inward. It promotes balance, alignment and correct posture. This posture creates a weight distribution similar to a proper stance during the golf game. Pressing into the feet and feeling the support of the earth establishes grounding.

Stand erect, with your feet in line with the hips, or together. The feet should be parallel with your toes pointing forward.

On the balls of your feet, slowly shift your weight backward and forward until you reach a point of equilibrium.

Press your feet into the ground. Slightly lift the arches of the feet and the kneecaps.

Engage the muscles of your thighs.

Tuck in your pelvis, neither arching nor rounding the back.

Lift your chest and lengthen the spine.

Draw your shoulders back and down, away from the ears.

Raise your head to the ceiling. The head should be aligned with your spine.

Relax and level your jaw. Take a moment to get centered and establish Ujjayi breathing.

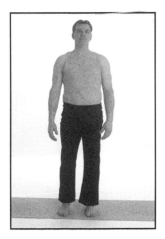

2. SWINGING WITH "HA"

The swinging action of this exercise rotates the torso and spine, loosens the muscles of the shoulders and warms the shoulder joints. This movement serves to bring awareness to the body regions that are most involved in the golf swing. It brings heat to the upper body. The vocalization of the "Ha" works the lungs and diaphragm and gives an audible cue for matching movement and breath, a key feature of mind-body exercise. The coordination of breath and movement is an essential part of the entire practice, reminding the golfer to breathe and nourish the body in play. Forcibly exhaling air clears the lungs and bronchial tubes.

Begin standing with your feet hip width apart and the knees slightly bent.

Press into your feet, establishing a connection with the ground.

Inhale and swing your arms loosely to one side.

Exhale with a "Ha" sound, through your open mouth, swinging the arms and torso to the other side.

Remember to keep your hips facing forward, and rotate from the torso up to look behind you as you swing.

As you progress in the exercise, swing your arms higher and with more energy.

When your warm-up is complete, gradually slow the movements until stopped.

Repeat 21 times to the left and 21 times to the right.

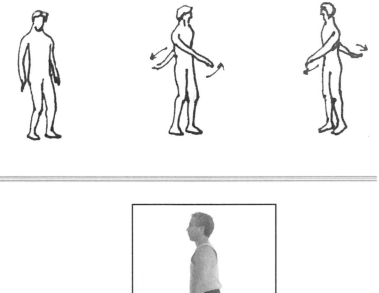

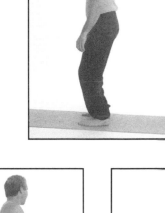

3. SPINNING

Improving balance and equilibrium is key in conditioning for golf. This exercise helps the golfer gain stability in the game. While swinging the golf club, a weight shift occurs. The golfer must remain steady and balanced throughout. While putting, the golfer also needs to be steady and grounded, relaxing the greater part of the body. Working through dizziness, induced through spinning helps the mind and body to become more stable.

Stand with your feet parallel, about 6 inches apart.

Extend your arms fully to the sides, so they are parallel to the floor and straight.

Turn your whole body clockwise, picking up your feet as you spin. (Do not fix your eyes on any one point, but allow your eyes to look ahead of your movement as you spin.)

Gradually slow down the spinning and come to rest.

Start with 7-10 repetitions and increase by 3 repetitions every three days. Very gradually build up to 21, or to your individual limit.

4. WOOD CHOPPER

The movement of working the legs, arms, and torso quickly warms the body and increases the heart rate. Movement of the limbs also dynamically stretches the hips, legs, arms, shoulders, back and spine. Swinging the arms through the legs releases tension in the arms and shoulders. The upward movement of the body works to strengthen the back and legs. The slightly aerobic nature of the exercise benefits the heart so that walking 18 holes becomes a little less strenuous.

Start with your feet slightly wider than hip width apart.

Clasp your hands above your head, interlacing your fingers.

Inhale through your nose and exhale through the mouth.

Swing your arms and head down through bent legs.

Inhale as you bring your body upright to standing, and bring your arms up above head. Straighten your legs.

Repeat 21 times.

5. CHAIR POSE

The chair pose is a powerful pose that is like sitting in an imaginary chair. It promotes strong ankles and legs and releases stiffness in the shoulders. The body quickly warms with this posture, while the abdominal and back muscles are toned. An element of balance is needed to hold the pose steadily.

Stand with your feet about 6 inches apart, or together if you feel well balanced.

Bend your knees and lower your buttocks back as if sitting in a chair.

The hips should not drop below knee level.

Keep your knees facing forward and your torso upright, eyes looking forward.

Engage the muscles of your buttocks and inner thighs, feeling the strength in your legs.

Raise your arms until they are shoulder height and level with the ground directly in front of you, or straight up overhead, close to the ears.

Breathe deeply and slowly.

Focus on your feet pressing into the earth, and on the upper body reaching up from the waist.

To come out of the pose, inhale, straighten your legs and lower the arms.

Repeat 7 times, holding for three breaths each time.

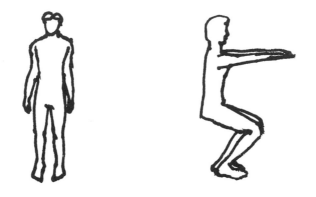

6. UPWARD FACING DOG / DOWNWARD FACING DOG

Performed in a dynamic fashion, these poses stretch and strengthen alternate planes of the body, front and back. They also revitalize the entire body and increase stamina. The downward facing dog pose is a weight-bearing posterior stretch that increases energy in the body. It strengthens the legs and ankles, as well as the arms. Any stiffness in the heels or calf muscles is relieved. Shoulder tension is eliminated. The inverted nature of the pose helps to rejuvenate the mind and relieve fatigue. The spine is elongated.

Moving into the upward facing dog pose works the abdominal muscles as well as the arms, wrists, elbows and shoulders. It removes stiffness in the back of the body. The chest region is expanded and lung capacity is increased. The downward movement of the hips promotes blood flow to the pelvis, a key region in the execution of the golf swing.

Begin this exercise in a tabletop position, on your hands and knees.

Place your hands directly under your shoulders and your knees under your hips.

Walk your hands 3-5 inches forward.

Pressing your hands flat into the mat with index fingers pointing forward, lift your hips high into the air while straightening the legs and back.

Reach your chest toward your legs.

Lengthen and align your arms and back to form an inverted V position. If your spine cannot straighten into the inverted V position, then bend your knees slightly to elongate the back more.

Gaze toward your knees or navel.

Breathe deeply throughout the movement.

To move into upward facing dog position, lower the hips while keeping the arms and legs straight, coming into a push-up position.

Then continue to lower your hips, engaging the buttocks and ham string muscles to protect the lower back.

Look forward, open your chest, drawing the shoulders down and back. Press strongly into your hands and balls of the feet.

Breathe deeply.

To return to downward dog pose, push down into your hands and raise the hips up to the inverted V position.

Repeat 7 times and gradually increase to 21 repetitions.
When repetitions are complete, come back to your hands and knees.

7. BELLOWS BREATH

With this pranayama, air is energetically drawn in and out of the body as with a blacksmith's bellows. The motion of the arms loosens the shoulders. Any stale air is removed from the lungs with the downward motion of the arms. The body is flooded with oxygen (prana) as toxins and carbon dioxide are expelled. Bellows breath has a calming yet energizing effect. Bellows breath is done with normal breath (not Ujjayi breath).

In a comfortable, seated position raise the hands to shoulder height, fingers in soft fists facing forward, with elbows bent resting close to the rib cage.

Take one normal breath in and out as a transition.

Vigorously extend your arms straight up on an inhalation through the nose and open the hands with the palms facing forward and fingers fully extended.

Close your hands as you pull the arms down to the starting position, simultaneously exhaling forcefully through the nose.

Squeeze your upper arms into the rib cage with the lowering motion.

Repeat the same raising and lowering action of the arms, while strongly inhaling and exhaling through the nose.

Repeat 21 times for two rounds.

NOTES

Chapter 8: Asanas

The word asana is Sanskrit for "seat". Asanas are the third branch of yoga. Asanas refer to the postures or poses that make up the path of hatha yoga. Health and flexibility in the body comes through practice with the poses. The asanas are convenient in that they can be performed anywhere. The limbs of your body provide the weight and counter-weight for practice. They bring agility, balance, endurance and vitality to the body. They have evolved over the years to exercise every muscle, nerve and gland of the body. Asanas are not just focused on the structural groups of the body, but they also address the nerves, internal organs, blood flow and energy.

Through practicing the poses you can teach your mind to stay focused, yet remain calm. With asanas your mind can be quiet through possible adversity.

Yoga Exercises

Section	No.	Technique	Duration Minutes	Cumulative Time
Warm-up (7)	1	Mountain Pose	1:00	1
	2	Swinging with Ha	2:00	3
	3	Spinning	1:00	4
	4	Wood Chopper	1:00	5
	5	Chair Pose	1:00	6
	6	Upward / Downward Facing Dog	2:00	8
	7	Bellows Breath	1:00	9
Asanas (11)	**8**	**Revolving Triangle**	**1:00**	**10**
	9	**Standing Yoga Mudra**	**1:00**	**11**
	10	**Tree Pose**	**2:00**	**13**
	11	**Spinal Twist and Hold**	**2:00**	**15**
	12	**Cobbler's Stretch**	**2:00**	**17**
	13	**Pigeon Stretch**	**2:00**	**19**
	14	**Snake Pose**	**2:00**	**21**
	15	**Sitting Still MID-POINT**	**3:00**	**24**
	16	**Sun Salutations**	**10:00**	**34**
	17	**Eye Exercise**	**1:00**	**35**
	18	**Neck Rolls**	**2:00**	**37**
Integration (3)	19	Alternative Nostril Breathing	2:00	39
	20	Three Stage Breathing	2:00	41
	21	Corpse Pose	4:00	45

After the warm-up, you are ready to begin the ASANAS, poses (#8-18)

8. REVOLVING TRIANGLE

This is an intense pose that develops strength and flexibility in the legs, especially in the hamstrings. The rotation of the torso stretches the spine and the muscles, front to back. There is an increase in blood flow to the lower back region. The abdominal organs are stimulated and toned, while the hip muscles are stretched and strengthened. There is also an element of balance to the posture that adds to the challenge and improves concentration.

Begin in Mountain Pose. Spread your legs about one leg length apart with feet facing forward, and raise the arms to the side at shoulder height.

Turn your torso to the left and fold forward at the hips, reaching the right hand down toward the left shin or ankle.

As your right arm reaches across and down, the left arm reaches upward.

Keep pressing down into both feet equally.

Rotate your torso with this movement, accentuating the twist by raising the left arm up and right arm down.

Turn your neck so you can look up to the raised hand. Continue to breathe deeply.

To come out of the pose, press down into the feet and inhale as you raise your arms back to shoulder height and as the torso returns to the upright position.

Let the breathing come back to normal.

Repeat the posture to the right side, 7 breaths on each side.

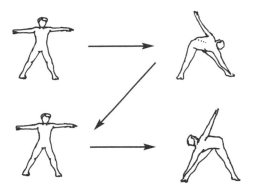

9. STANDING YOGA MUDRA

This posture combines an excellent shoulder stretch with leg strength-ening. The entire backside of the body, especially the legs and lower back, are stretched. While opening the front of the body and lengthening the backs of the legs circulation to the legs, torso and brain is increased. The positioning of the head below the heart symbolizes the importance of feeling and compassion.

Start in Mountain Pose.

Inhale while reaching your arms to your sides and back, interlacing your fingers behind your back, with the palms together.

Roll your shoulders down and back, away from the ears.

Slowly lift your arms up and away from the back, squeezing the shoulder blades together and expanding your chest region. At the same time bend forward at the hips over your legs, reaching the abdomen into the thighs. Bend your knees as needed. Reach your arms up and away from your back. (Do not move so far into the pose that you prevent deep breathing).

To come out of the pose, slowly roll up from the base of your spine as you raise your torso. Simultaneously lower the arms, bringing the head up last.

Repeat 2 times for 4 breaths each or 1 time for 7 breaths.

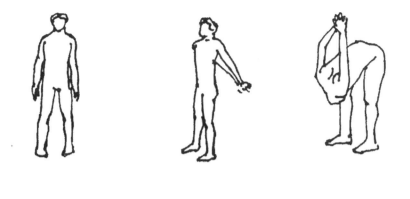

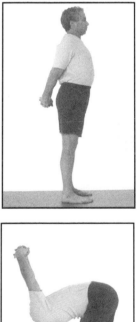

10. TREE POSE

Tree pose cultivates balance and composure. The practitioner challenges the body by standing on just one leg. Focusing on the connection to the earth, while remaining light and lifted upward, will help achieve this pose. Increased strength is also an important benefit. Imbalances in leg strength are quickly revealed when attempting this pose. Pressing the knee to the outside of the body develops hip flexibility.

Stand erect in Mountain Pose with your feet together or as near as possible. Your feet should be parallel and the toes spread. Find a stationary focal point in front of you, at eye level.

Bring your hands in front of the chest in prayer position, palms and fingers together with the thumbs pointing to the sternum.

Press into your right foot, keeping the leg straight and active, then slowly raise the left foot.

Place the bottom of your left foot to the inside of the right calf, lower thigh, or upper thigh.

Reach long through your torso, while grounding into the standing leg. [Be satisfied with any of the three foot positions on the standing leg. It may take a few weeks before you may attempt to rest your foot on the upper thigh.]

Open your left leg out to the side, while pressing the bottom of the left foot into the right leg.

Tuck in your tailbone, and, breathing deeply, gradually practice to raise your arms in an open V-position just like branches of a tree.

To come out of the pose, rotate your raised leg to the front with the knee still bent, lower the foot slowly to the ground, returning your hands to prayer position.

Repeat on the other side.

Hold the pose for 7 breaths on each side.

11. SPINAL TWIST AND HOLD

The asana of turning the trunk in a spiraling movement from the hips is very effective in relieving backaches and headaches, as well as relieving stiffness in the neck and shoulders. The spine becomes flexible, and the hips move more easily. Twisting mimics the motion of the full golf swing and prepares the body to perform the swing with greater ease and less chance of injury.

Sit in a simple sitting position, your legs comfortably crossed, on the floor.

Keep your back straight, and your head lifted, with the shoulders rolled down and back.

Bend your arms and place your hands on the shoulders with the fingers to the front and the thumb to the back.

Inhale and exhale with a twist to one side.

Keep your elbows aligned with the shoulders.

Continue inhaling and exhaling while twisting from side to side. (Both hips should remain grounded through the motion, and the upper arms should remain parallel to the ground.)

After 21 twists, release your hands from the shoulders. Place the right hand on the left knee and the left hand on the floor behind the back for support.

Hold the final twist position to the left side and gaze behind you.

Breathe deeply for 7 breaths as you hold the twist.

Slowly release the left twist and repeat a single twist to the right side for 7 breaths.

12. COBBLER'S STRETCH

In this position the pelvis, hips, and back receive a deep stretch and get a plentiful supply of blood. The inner thighs, muscles around the hip joint and the hamstrings become more flexible. The back and the spine are strengthened.

Sit upright and bring the soles of your feet together in front of your body. The feet can be up to one foot from the pelvis. (Sitting on the edge of a pillow or cushion will help keep the back straight by tilting the pelvis slightly forward.)

Press the heels of your feet together, while relaxing the knees open to the sides. Hold your feet with your hands.

Reach your upper body long, then, exhaling, come forward, keeping the spine elongated. (Do not round your back or collapse the front of the body.)

Lead with the navel and chest, and keep the buttocks on the floor.

Press out and down with your legs.

Breathe deeply in this position while you relax your upper body over the feet.

Inhale and return to an upright sitting position.

Repeat once for 7 breaths.

  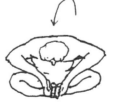

13. PIGEON STRETCH

The single leg pigeon stretch is an excellent hip opener. It gives an intense stretch to the hips, buttocks, and thighs, as well as the spine. The pose stretches and strengthens the back. It stretches and relaxes the knees and legs. Its emphasis on flexibility in the hip area makes it ideal for the golfer.

Begin in table position, on your hands and knees, hands under shoulder and knees under hips.

Bend your right knee and draw it forward between the hands.

Turn your right heel slightly in, toward the left wrist, and place the bent leg on the floor.

Lower your hips to the floor.

Reach your left leg straight back with the knee facing down, pointing the left toes. (A small cushion can be placed under the right hip if it is not settled to the floor. Make sure that there is no pain in the knee.)

Sit up tall in this position, gently arching back and looking forward. While exhaling, come down on the hands or forearms, or extend the arms and torso forward over the bent leg. Breathe deeply in this position.

To come out of the pose, walk your hands backwards under the shoulders. Press down with the hands, and lift the bent knee off the floor, returning to the tabletop position.

Hold this position for 7 breaths and repeat on the other side.

14. SNAKE POSE

This pose is a variation of the conventional cobra pose. It is an excellent back, buttocks and leg strengthener. It additionally focuses on loosening the shoulders and opening the chest. The spine is stretched back and becomes more elastic. As all of the muscles of the back are strengthened, the abdominal region is also stimulated and expanded.

Lie full length on the floor; face down on your stomach. Turn your chin forward, and place your arms to the sides of the body. (The legs should be a few inches apart, knees down, and the toes pointed.)

Press your hips and pelvis into the floor.

Reach your hands behind your back and interlace the fingers.

Open your chest and keep the neck elongated.

Inhale as you raise your upper and lower body off the floor at the same time, balancing on the lower abdomen.

Squeeze your shoulder blades together.

Contract your buttock muscles, and press the tailbone under, as you raise the legs with pointed toes. Keep the knees straight. (Do not strain the back.)

Stay in this position for 20 to 30 seconds, breathing evenly.

Lower your body to the floor on an exhalation and unclasp the hands. Turn the head to one side and rest. Allow your breathing to come back to normal.

Repeat the pose 2 times and gradually work to holding for 7 breaths.

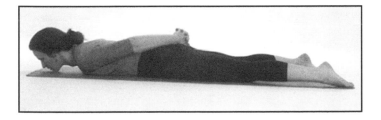

15. SITTING STILL

Sitting still (Jivana mudra) is the symbol of higher consciousness. A mudra is a body position symbol that serves as a metaphor for concepts that can be experienced but cannot be seen. A mudra redirects energy within your body. It also serves as an aid to concentration during meditation and relaxation practices.

Sitting comfortably with your spine erect and shoulders relaxed, lay your hands face up on the tops of your thighs.

Actively stretch out all your fingers, then close the index finger tips down to meet the thumb tips.

Connect to a higher cause. Set your intent to as high an ideal and noble cause as you can imagine.

(You may want to hope and pray for world peace, harmony among all of mankind, contentment and prosperity or eradication of all poverty and disease. Then hope that your intent is going to set everything right in the world. Let that sense of hope transform into a feeling that bathes you completely inside with immense satisfaction. Imagine that you are prepared and able to extend this intent of yours everywhere. This bath of satisfaction is your inter-connection to the highest cause of the moment.)

Every time you sit still, repeat the above with a different intention or ideal.

(If you notice that your fingers begin to curl up or drift apart, simply bring fingers back into the original starting position.)

16. SUN SALUTATIONS

Sun salutations warm and strengthen the whole body, while synchroniz-ing the breath with movement. Sun salutations are approximately 12 postures performed in sequence. The poses are performed according to the principle of pose and counterpose. There is a continual flow of movement, thereby repre-senting a dynamic approach to the asana. Made up of both forward and back-bending poses, this sequence creates a perfect balance of strength and flexibili-ty to the musculature of the whole front and back of the body. These poses also work the body building endurance and coordination.

Begin standing straight and tall in Mountain Pose, then bring your hands in the prayer position. With your thumbs hooked, inhale and reach the arms forward, then over the head. Be sure to coordinate the movement exactly with the breath.

Slightly arch the back, tucking the tailbone under, and squeeze the buttock muscles. Lengthen the front of the body.

Hinging at your hips, exhale and fold your torso over your legs. Reach your arms forward and down. The knees can be bent as the abdomen comes to the thighs. Make the movement smooth.

Bend your knees and place the fingertips or hands flat on either side of the feet.

Lunge your right leg straight back, landing on the ball of the foot. Keep the front leg so that the knee remains over the ankle. Keep the back leg straight with your knee off the floor.

Bring the front leg back alongside the back leg. Lift the hips and lengthen the back and arms for a downward dog pose.

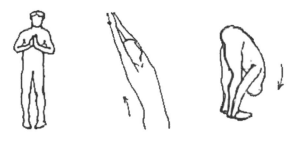

16. SUN SALUTATIONS (CONT.)

Lower your hips and bring the body forward into a high plank position. The body should be level and parallel to the floor.

Bring your hips even lower with the chest moving through the arms, into upward dog position. Keep the legs and arms straight and strong, as you lift the hips back up into the downward dog position once again.

Bend your right knee into the chest and swing the leg forward, placing the foot between the hands into a high lunge pose. Bring the back leg forward alongside the front leg and fold forward over your legs.

With your thumbs hooked, inhale reaching forward and up. Pressing down with the legs, raise the body up slowly, arching slightly back.

Exhale and return the hands to prayer position.

Repeat 4 to 5 times for each leg.

17. Eye Exercise

The late Swami Sivananda considered the eyes to be the fastest route to bringing the mind into focus. He taught the importance of working with the eyes, exercising them and providing them with conscious relaxation. Eye asanas stimulate the muscles and nerves of the eyes. They relieve eye fatigue and strain. They sharpen vision. The importance of the eyes in golf is evident in targeting the ball to the hole. Judgments of distance and angles are necessary elements of the game.

Sit in a relaxed position, either in a chair or on the floor.

With your eyes open, the head and neck still, envision a clock face. Raise your eyeballs to twelve o'clock. Hold them there for a second then lower them to six o'clock. Hold them there for a second, also. Continue moving the eyeballs up and down 7 times, without blinking if possible. Follow this exercise with movements in the horizontal direction, from nine o'clock to three o'clock, 7 times. Your gaze should be steady and relaxed.

Once you finish these movements, rub your palms together to generate heat and gently cup your eyes without pressing. First close, then open your eyes to relax in complete darkness. Breathe in and out with relaxation.

Keep your eyes completely covered, allowing no light to filter in between each set.

Conclude the asana with 7 full circles in clockwise and counter-clock wise direction, as though circling the rim of the clock.

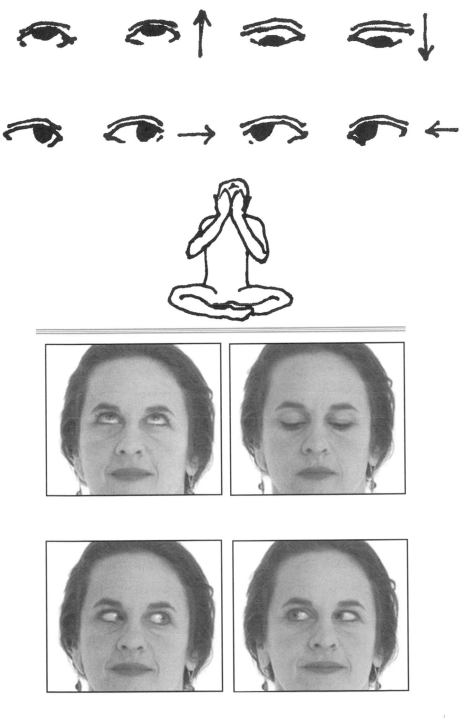

18. NECK ROLLS

This exercise stretches and relaxes the neck and upper shoulders. Stress in these areas inhibits the free flow of energy in the golf swing.

Be sure to move slowly and breathe deeply with these movements.

Sitting in a comfortable position, inhale.

As you exhale, lower your chin slowly to the chest. Keep the shoulders moving down, away from the ears.

Slowly turn your head in a counter-clockwise direction moving the chin to a position over the right shoulder. Roll your head back without collapsing the neck. Keep the neck open and long.

Turn your chin over to the left side.

3 circles counter-clockwise and clockwise, slowly.

  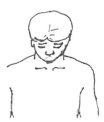

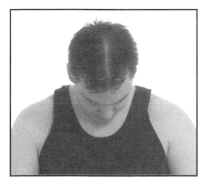 

Chapter 9: Integration

The integration portion of the program refers to the time you take at the end of practice to allow your body to absorb and assimilate the benefits of the yoga practice. It is a time to turn inward, relax, and renew. It is time to let flow out of your body any remaining stress or tension. Integration relieves fatigue and restores your energy.

Yoga Exercises

Section	No.	Technique	Duration Minutes	Cumulative Time
Warm-up (7)	1	Mountain Pose	1:00	1
	2	Swinging with Ha	2:00	3
	3	Spinning	1:00	4
	4	Wood Chopper	1:00	5
	5	Chair Pose	1:00	6
	6	Upward / Downward Facing Dog	2:00	8
	7	Bellows Breath	1:00	9
Asanas (11)	8	Revolving Triangle	1:00	10
	9	Standing Yoga Mudra	1:00	11
	10	Tree Pose	2:00	13
	11	Spinal Twist and Hold	2:00	15
	12	Cobbler's Stretch	2:00	17
	13	Pigeon Stretch	2:00	19
	14	Snake Pose	2:00	21
	15	Sitting Still **MID-POINT**	3:00	24
	16	Sun Salutations	10:00	34
	17	Eye Exercise	1:00	35
	18	Neck Rolls	2:00	37
Integration (3)	**19**	**Alternative Nostril Breathing**	**2:00**	**39**
	20	**Three Stage Breathing**	**2:00**	**41**
	21	**Corpse Pose**	**4:00**	**45**

19. ALTERNATE NOSTRIL BREATHING

Alternate Nostril Breathing is a pranayama technique that balances the hemispheres of the brain, calming and relaxing the nervous system. Alternate Nostril Breathing helps to balance the body and mind, while it also soothes and calms the nerves, leaving one feeling mentally alert and relaxed.

Sit in a simple sitting position with your legs gently crossed.

Using your right hand, let your index and third fingers rest gently near the eyebrow center.

Bring your thumb lightly to the right nostril and the tip of the ring finger in a ready position near the left nostril.

Bow your head slightly forward and let your awareness turn inward.

Breath should be slow, even, and deep.

1. Close your right nostril with the thumb, and inhale completely through the left nostril, using regular breath (not Ujjayi).

2 Close your left nostril with the ring finger and exhale through the right nostril for four counts.

3. Inhale through your right nostril, close the right nostril with the thumb, and exhale through the left nostril for four counts.

This completes one cycle. Continue with these for 7 cycles.

The counting during inhalation and exhalation can be omitted while you are learning this technique, until a comfortable rhythm and pattern of breathing is established. Once you have become adept at the basic form of alternate nostril breathing, the counting can be included. The counts can be gradually increased as well. Do not increase the length of the count if you have the slightest feeling of strain or discomfort. Relaxation should not be sacrificed.

As you proceed with the cycles, be careful that your hand is not pulling the head off center. Make sure that your chest remains upright, while the head bows slightly. Check your body alignment every few cycles. Be sure that the fingers are not over pressing the nostrils. The septum of your nose should not be pushed off center.

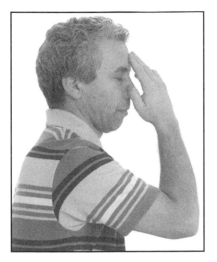
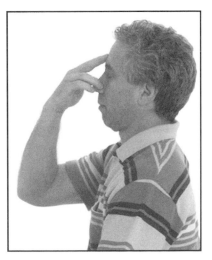

20. THREE STAGE BREATHING

Three-stage breathing increases lung capacity and calms the body. It is a wonderful diaphragmatic breathing technique that replenishes one's energy. Dividing the focus of the breath into three areas expands the lung capacity and lengthens the exhalation, which, in turn, deepens the resulting inhalation of breath. Breath awareness and quality are improved by focusing on three different regions involved in the breathing process. Three-stage breathing is an effective technique to reduce any anxiety in the body.

Sit comfortably, with your spine erect, or lie on your back on the floor.

Place your hands above the navel center near the diaphragm.

Focus on the feeling of your belly moving with the breath.

Using Ujjayi breath, breathe in for four counts, hold for four counts, and breathe out for six counts, concentrating on bringing the breath deep into your belly. Repeat for seven breaths.

Next, place your hands on either sides of the rib cage and repeat the same set of breaths. (Using Ujjayi breath, breathe in for four counts, hold for four counts, and breathe out for six counts). Focus on filling the belly first, then the mid section of the chest, expanding the ribs.

As you exhale, empty your lungs from the middle region first, then the belly region. Repeat for seven breaths.

Finally, repeat with your hands up in the region of the sternum. As you inhale, breathe deep down into the belly, then fill the middle chest and finally bring the upper region of the lungs into the breath.

Exhale in the same order, beginning with the upper lung and moving down. Let all the air be released slowly through the nose, as you empty your lungs as completely as possible from the top to the bottom. Repeat for seven breaths.

Relax with the palms of hands on thighs, if in sitting position.

Lower, middle, upper lungs: approximately 7 breaths each.

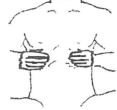

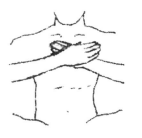

21. CORPSE POSE

Any and every yoga session should be completed with a period of relaxation. It can be considered the counter pose for the whole program. Corpse pose relieves any fatigue associated with the asana practice. It quiets the nervous system and allows for the integration of the postures. The breathing relaxes, while the entire body rests in a reclined position on the floor. The eyes are closed. The mind also "rests", remaining free from concern but observant. A deep level of rest is attained, accompanied by an awareness of the process. This meditative state leaves one feeling refreshed and energized. Corpse pose is the classic relaxation pose that traditionally completes all hatha yoga sessions.

Lie on your back on the floor. The body should be symmetrically aligned and at rest. Close your eyes.

Draw your shoulders down, away from the ears.

Place your legs slightly wider than hip width apart and relax the feet outward.

Move the arms slightly away from the body, and rest the hands with the palms upward. Feel the chest gently opening.

Once you are satisfied with the alignment of your body, remain in that position for the duration of the relaxation session. Notice the feeling of support that the earth provides, and feel your body relax.

During the relaxation, you can observe how your body feels after the practice. Observe each part of the body and let go of any residual tension.

Take note of your breathing. Take a few deep abdominal breaths, releasing any leftover stress. Let the breathing become quiet. Observe your normal inhalation and your exhalation. There is no need to perform Ujjayi breath during this pose. Let any thoughts that enter your mind flow out of your mind.

To come out of relaxation, slowly deepen your breathing. As consciousness returns, begin to move your fingers and toes. Stretch and move in any way that feels right to you. Slowly bend your knees and roll to the right side. Rest there for a few moments. Bring yourself gently to a seated position, and remain there for a moment or two. Then slowly get up to conclude this practice session.

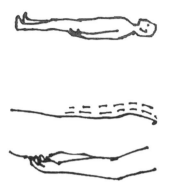

Take note of your breathing

PART THREE

Chapter 10: Om or Aum

At the beginning of the yoga program, the golfer can silence internal chatter by reciting attentively the word **OM**, pronounced as AUM. Dating back to Vedic times, Indian chanting comes from a tradition that believes in the creative power of sound and its potential to transport us to an expanded state of awareness. The rishis, or ancient seers, taught that all of creation is a manifestation of the primordial sound **OM**. It is the original and most powerful chant or mantra of the yogic tradition. Reflected in an interpretation of the word universe, **OM** is the seed sound of all other sounds. All other mantras are derived from **OM**.

OM is considered to be the most natural sound that can be uttered. It is prominent in many languages and in many contexts. OM is also known as *pranava*, that which permeates life, or runs through the *prana* or breath. OM is the sound of the divine, the infinite, and the universe.

OM consists of *A, U, M*. According to the rules of Sanskrit phonology, *A* and *U* joined together are *O*. The sounds of the letters in Aum - *A-U-M* - each have their own individual attributes, and, when brought together, have additional meanings. The A represents fire, the earth, the past and intuition. It is grounded in the self as manifested in the waking state. The *U* corresponds to wind, the atmosphere, the present and intellect. It represents the dream and the psychic or astral worlds. The *M* represents the sun, the sky, the future and thoughts. It denotes the absolute self, underlying the chaotic state and representing the entire unknown, the deep sleep. *OM* can be chanted at any stage of the outlined yoga program --- at the beginning, the halfway point, or the end of practice. It is customary to begin and end a yoga practice with chanting *OM* three times. It serves to begin the centering process and to acknowledge our place in the infinite.

There are three stages of vibrations in the chanting of **OM** or AUM:

- To chant the AUM, begin by inhaling deeply.
- On exhalation make the sound *aaaahh*. It will feel as if it is coming from your abdomen.
- Next make the sound *uuuuh*: it will feel as though it is coming from the chest.
- Finally, make the sound *mmmm* with closed lips. It will feel as if it is coming from the head.

Putting the three sounds together, inhale, then, while exhaling, chant *aaaahh-uuuuh-mmmm,* **OM** or AUM. End the session by repeating it three times.

NOTES

EPILOGUE

The practice of yoga can be a great complement to your game of golf. Both yoga and golf are excellent physical activities for people of all ages and levels of fitness. Yoga highlights the principles of physical and mental conditioning that are beneficial to you, the golfer, and to every athlete. The mind-body integration of conditioning through yoga allows the player to achieve both physical and mental benefits.

Superior physical condition of the whole body is possible with yoga. While your body becomes strong and flexible through yoga, your balance and alignment are improved, your physical awareness increases, and your ability to adjust posture and movements appropriately in the game becomes greater and more natural.

Through your breath, the mind and body can form a connection. Deep breathing brings physical benefits by increasing energy and nourishing the body. Breathing through adversities keeps the mind calm, creating patience and acceptance of self. Concentration on breathing helps the golfer reduce distractions, both inside and out.

Conscious yoga practice teaches you how to relax while involved in play, letting your physical conditioning come to fruition. Not allowing negative emotions and thoughts to lead to aggression or disappointment during golf increases your enjoyment of the game. The moment-to-moment focus of yoga practice encourages the golfer to let the game, and life, unfold.

$$************************************$$

Become aware of the thoughts that may contribute to fear of failure or fear of embarrassment. Let go of over-analyzing the game and let the body do what it has been trained to do. Let go of the "I should haves" between shots. Allow the conscious mind to quiet, so that the subconscious conditioning can come through and help you play the game.

Experience mental clarity and a sense of calm peace on the greens. Coordinate your mind and body through the lessons of yoga. When faced by hazards and other physical distractions on the course, block them out of your mind. Know that the obstacles will fade, if you are focusing on the target instead. Focus on what you want to do, rather than on what you do not want to happen.

Focus on the ball, then on the target. Do not be controlled by fear or concern about how the shot is going to come out, before it is fully executed. Concentrate on your breathing, posture, and balance. Bring the principles of yoga into the game of golf.

By not focusing so much on the outcome of the game, you can detach from the game and lighten up. Defer calculation of the score until the end of the game, so as to remove some of the pressure, and allow yourself to play the game, stroke by stroke. Let go of each shot after it is executed, and clear your mind of the game between shots to reduce anxiety and the possible frustration of the game.

Use breathing techniques to relax on the golf course during a pre-game or pre-shot ritual to prepare yourself mentally and physically. Practice deep diaphragmatic breathing to bring calm to your body and connect to the breath, allowing yourself to clear your conscious mind. Mindfully breathe to dispel any fear response that may arise. As you walk to your ball, just breathe in and breathe out, using deep meditative breaths. Focus on the feeling of the earth between each step, the shades of green in the landscape, the shapes of the clouds or trees. Feel the sun or wind on your skin. Think and move with calm clarity. Be one with the game. Enjoy your game of golf. You have found *The Missing Peace.*

****

****

GLOSSARY

ASANA

Asana originally referred only to the various sitting positions for meditation. In literal terms it means a "seat." Asana implies an "easy pose" or "comfortable position." In Tantra and Hatha Yoga, asana applies to all of the technical and physical positions of the body.

ASTANGA

Astanga are literally "eight limbs," meaning the eight parts into which the sage Patanjali organized yoga. The Eight Limbs, or branches, are a progressive series of steps or disciplines, which purify the body and mind, ultimately leading to enlightenment.

They are: Yamas (restraints, moral injunctions), Niyamas (observances, ethical precepts), Asanas (postures), Pranayama (regulation or control of the breath), Pratyahara (withdrawal of the senses), Dharana (concentration), Dhyana (meditation), and Samadhi (the super-conscious state, one with the Self or God).

CORPSE POSE

"Savasana" in Sanskrit or corpse pose, is the classical relaxation pose and traditionally completes all hatha yoga sessions. In this pose, lying supine on the floor, the body is symmetrically aligned, yet at rest.

HATHA YOGA

Most of the yoga postures familiar to westerners are part of Hatha Yoga, the physical discipline of yoga. Technically, the term means "self-integration through the union of opposites." Hatha Yoga aims to eliminate any false sense of duality within the practitioner. The physical postures, or asanas, help to integrate the body, mind and spirit when performed with mindfulness and specific breathing techniques, "pranayama."

JIVANA

Jivana means "life."

MUDRA

Literally mudra means a "seal" or a sealing posture, usually of the hands. It refers to any of a number of muscular contractions used to control the positioning and movement of "prana" or the life force.

OM OR AUM

Om, pronounced as "aum" is a mantra, which is described as the primordial sound; the sound through which the manifest world comes into being. In some Upanishads, the ancient Hindu texts, it is written that enlightenment may come from chanting this mantra alone.

PATANJALI

Patanjali is the author of the Yoga Sutras. He lived sometime between 200 B.C. and 200 A.D., but the exact date is unknown. Patanjali traveled throughout much of India, studying and analyzing what different practitioners and teachers were doing under the name of "yoga." Patanjali did not contribute any new ideas or practices to yoga. Rather, he provided a valuable structural analysis of yoga during his time.

PRADIPIKA
Pradipika is one of the earliest treatises on Hatha Yoga. All modern yoga books are based on it. The Hatha Yoga path was outlined by 14 great beings, among them, yogis called Siddhas, Matsyendranath, (his disciple) and Gorakshanath, in the Hatha Yoga Pradipika, an ancient text.

PRANA
Prana has several connotations. It refers to the vital energy of life, the breath, vitality, spirit, life force and/or soul.

PRANAVA
Pravana is the sacred monosyllable Om.

PRANAYAMA
Breathing exercises are called Pranayamas, which means to control the Prana, or the subtle energy of the vital breath. Control of the prana leads to control of the mind.

RISHI
Rishi is a sage or a wise person.

SANSKRIT
Sanskrit is the ancient spiritual language of India, dating back 4000 to 7000 years and brought to formal perfection.

TABLETOP
Tabletop is the asana in which the practitioner is positioned on the hands and knees, with the wrists under the shoulders, the knees under the hips and the back flat.

TANTRA
Tantra is the yoga pathway of ritual. Those who embrace this path find celebration and ritual to be sacred.

UJJAYI
Ujjayi breath is a type of pranayama also known as "victorious breath." Such breathing is done in and out through the nose with the contraction of the epiglottis at the back of the throat. The throat position is similar to that of whispering. The resulting breath is slow, steady, and audible.

VEDA
Veda is the highest authority among the Aryans of India. It refers to "revealed wisdom," specifically one of the four collections that comprise the Hindu scriptures. The Rig Veda is the oldest, followed by the Sama, Atharva, and Yajur Vedas.

YOGA
Yoga is one of six orthodox philosophies evolved from ancient India. The word yoga has its roots in the word "yuj" of the Sanskrit language. Yoga means to bind, join, attach or yoke, as in binding man to the Universal, the Self, or the Divine.

YOGA MUDRA

Yoga Mudra is a yoga posture. It refers specifically to the asana in which the head is lower than the heart, symbolizing the subservience of the mind to the heart.

YOGA SUTRAS

Yoga Sutras are the writings of Patanjali. This work consists of 185 terse aphorisms on yoga, providing an excellent treatise on the subject of yoga. Divided into four parts, Yoga Sutras specifically and respectively explain dealing with samadhi, how yoga is attained, the powers the seeker may encounter in the quest, and the state of absolution.

YOGI

A practitioner of yoga (female: yogini). In general terms it implies a sage.

YOGIC

Yogic pertains to yoga.

NOTES

NOTES

NOTES

NOTES

NOTES